JEWS OF CONSCIENCE

RELIGION IN A GLOBALISING WORLD SERIES

JEWS OF CONSCIENCE
Challenges and Choices

MARC H. ELLIS

WIPF & STOCK · Eugene, Oregon

Wipf and Stock Publishers
199 W 8th Ave, Suite 3
Eugene, OR 97401

Jews of Conscience
Challenges and Choices
By Ellis, Marc H.
Copyright©2009 by Ellis, Marc H.
ISBN 13: 978-1-5326-4693-5
Publication date 1/12/2018
Previously published by
Penerbit Universiti Sains Malaysia , 2009

CONTENTS

PREFACE TO THE 2018 REPRINT EDITION

AFTER I DELIVER A lecture on Israel and Palestine the question and answer time often becomes intense. Sometimes when emotions are high and the discussion becomes argumentative, I pause and ask the audience a question: "From what you've heard this evening, what do you want?" Once in a university setting, an exasperated faculty member, a well-meaning Christian, blurted out: "We want a good relationship with the Jewish community!" To which I responded: "Which part of the Jewish community?" In the ensuing back and forth it became clear that what she meant by good relations was the approval of the local rabbi and her congregation, even though the nearest Jewish synagogue was more than a hundred miles away.

Recently I lectured at a Mennonite seminary in a wonderful chapel that sported the incredible name, Chapel of the Sermon on the Mount. During the lecture I announced a need for a Center for Jews of Conscience. My announcement was strong, as if I had been thinking about such a center for a long time. When I reviewed my notes a few days later, I noticed the announcement wasn't in my prepared remarks. Rather the idea came to me as I spoke. Was it a subconscious response to the earlier desire for good relations with the Jewish community and my query as to which part? As our time together drew to a close, the moderator asked if I had a question for the audience. Without hesitation, I asked: "When will you start the Center for Jews of Conscience?"

When I suggested the center in my talk, I felt hopeful. When I called for the audience's response to my idea, I felt despair. I knew what the future needed, for Jews and for a solidarity with

Christians and Muslims as well. I knew that it was unlikely to come into being. A Center for Jews of Conscience will acknowledge a division within the Jewish community at large. It will be controversial. "Good relations" with the Jewish community will triumph.

The first edition of this book was published in 2009 by the Centre for Policy Research and International Studies at the Universiti Sains Malaysia. The book consisted of two of my lectures on Jews of Conscience and the challenge to Jewish life posed by the continuing expansion of Israel at the expense of Palestinian life and land and was aimed toward a Muslim audience, a controversial subject for the community at large. The book was introduced by the noted Malaysian scholar and activist, Dr. Chandra Muzaffar, who was then Noordin Sopiee Chair in Global Studies at the university. Muzaffar was quite effusive in his praise of my work but his general reason for publishing my lectures is more important: "These are ideas of great import in the context of a globalising world which resonate with societies everywhere, as conventional religious and ethnic boundaries yield to new notions of identity that are as yet amorphous and ambiguous."

These lectures also marked an important stage of my thinking about the emergence of Jews of Conscience. Earlier, I had explored what it meant to be Jewish after the Holocaust, but especially in light of the first Palestinian Uprising (1987-1993), I sharpened my understanding of the trajectory of Jewish history. The founding of the state of Israel occurred within the context of Jewish suffering and the need for empowerment after the destruction of European Jewry. Yet the Palestinians had been done a great wrong. Instead of correcting that wrong, however, Israel continued to pursue unjust policies toward Palestinians. The Palestinian Uprising was a moment of reckoning. What would Israel and Jews around the world choose for the future? The second reckoning came with the second Palestinian Uprising (2000-2005). During these years it became clear that Israel was bent on a permanent occupation of Palestine. Israel had no intention of righting the wrong it created. Israel, with the cooperation of the Jewish establishment in the United States, would not turn around.

I first wrote of Jews of Conscience during the second Palestinian Uprising, so the lectures featured in my book's first edition, delivered in Cairo in 2006 and Kuala Lumpur in 2008, represent a middle phase of my exploration. This second, expanded edition, features a third lecture I delivered in Jerusalem in 2017 on the occasion of the thirtieth anniversary of my *Toward a Jewish Theology of Liberation*. This later exploration is more developed and more dire. Taken together these lectures provide an outline of the difficult, almost impossible, future Jews face and the courage needed by non-Jews to accompany Jews in this difficult time if they are truly in solidarity with Jews and Jewish history. For as I point out in each of the lectures in different ways, though most disturbingly in my Jerusalem lecture, the only way forward for Jews and our allies is to understand in a radically altered form what 'good relations' with the Jewish community might mean in the future. For the occupation of Palestine by Israel is now permanent and the two other identifiable elements of the Jewish community, Constantinian Jews and Progressive Jews, are deeply culpable in the ongoing suffering of Palestinians. Both constituencies are enablers of the destruction of Palestine and thus, in my view, culpable in the end of ethical Jewish history.

What to do at the end of ethical Jewish history? During the years since my book's publication, there has been an explosion of the Jewish prophetic. Jews of Conscience have made their voice heard about the injustice committed by Israel against the Palestinian people. Jews of Conscience understand the deepest form of idolatry to be assimilation to injustice. More and more Jews feel that the final assimilation to injustice is right around the corner. As Jews of Conscience struggle against this assimilation, Jews find allies among those of different faith traditions. In turn, these interfaith encounters force the interfaith ecumenical dialogue to reckon with and ultimately abandon what has become a deal—one that requires Jewish and Christian silence on Palestine—and instead move toward a heartfelt and costly interfaith solidarity. More and more Christians, as well as others, realize that the only "good relations" that makes sense is between Jews and those who mirror the same values that other people of conscience embrace and embody.

What comes after the interfaith ecumenical deal collapses and the silence imposed therein is broken? Once Jews, Christians and others realize that Jews are neither innocent nor guilty, that there are parts to the Jewish community which are closer or further away from what each group identifies with, then "good relations" with the Jewish community can be critically assessed. The solidarity we need, the good relations we want, our true partnership, is with people of conscience across the board. Does it matter what faith or non-faith community we come from if we are practicing empire? If we are practicing community, the distinctions between communities is likewise blurred. Divided by symbols but united in the life we practice, what should bind us? Jews of Conscience are the Jewish part of the People of Conscience community that deserves a rightful place at the religious and political table.

In the pages that follow I propose a response to "good relations" with the Jewish community in a way that moves Jews and others forward in our search for justice, inclusiveness and an interfaith solidarity. As long as Jews of Conscience are left out in the cold when interfaith relations are discussed and embodied, Jewish dissenters, Palestinians and others trying to work for justice and reconciliation in Israel-Palestine will be denied their voice. Or rather, their voice, so alarming and insistent, will be kept at a distance that implicates us all. Instead, let us open our eyes and, like the prophets of old, proclaim justice for all in the land.

MARTIN BUBER, HANNAH ARENDT, EMMANUEL LEVINAS AND THE STATE OF ISRAEL
Charting a Way Forward?*

The questions related to Israel and the Palestinians are primarily political; they involve issues of history, land and power. In general, the struggle between Israel and the Palestinians is about land, land acquired, land won in war, land settled within and after war, disputed land. Land, of course, is intensely political and politicized. The international community with many and varied actors has, for close to a century, sought to negotiate issues between the two parties and to find a way out of an impasse that affects the Middle East region and the world in general. These negotiations, ongoing, ineffective and worsening in impact over time, continue into the 21st century. This, when the imbalance of power between Israel and the Palestinians, has never been more extreme. It is a cliché to say the political realities of Israel/Palestine couldn't be worse. They can be worse. They are becoming worse.

As a Jew, and a Jewish scholar of religion, I have been following this issue for decades. My first visit to the region was in 1973; I have been traveling regularly to Israel/Palestine since 1984, meeting and traveling with Palestinians then and since, with steady travel to the region during the late 1980s and beyond. I started writing on Israel/Palestine in 1984, publishing my first article on a Jewish theology of liberation. In 1987, I wrote my first book-length study of the conflict from the perspective of Jewish identity and religiosity; the third edition of *Toward a Jewish Theology of Liberation* was published in 2004.[1]

The subject of my remarks is not to flesh out the main arguments of my own writing but to share with you the search I have been involved in, albeit unsuccessfully, during these many years. In short, I, with some other Jews of Conscience, have been trying to

---

* A Lecture Sponsored by the Al Quds Club, American University of Cairo, Cairo, Egypt, December 12, 2006.

locate the possibilities within the Jewish tradition and history that would lead Israel to accommodate Palestinians with a full state along the internationally agreed upon borders of two states and also to confess to our attempt to dislocate, control and destroy the Palestinian population and leadership. These understandings are political in that they help rectify the situation the Palestinians find themselves in; they are also ethical and religious in the sense that they require that Israel understand what it has done and is doing, and change its ways as a way toward recovering the Jewish ethical tradition, and therefore our destiny as Jews to be an ethical people.

Though the latter points of my work are certainly contested—that they have failed completely is beyond doubt—and though politics of the matter is certainly more important, there is a dimension to my ethical search that is relevant to the history and politics of Israel and its relationship with Palestinians. This has to do with the narrative of Israel as presented by Israel itself, the narrative of Israel within European and American circles, Jewish and non-Jewish, and the philosophical and theological foundations of these narratives. Narratives are intensely political in that they allow or refuse certain assertions, advances and claims on the political.

In the case of Israel, the Holocaust and its interpretative framework are crucial to the argument for Israel and its power. So, too, is the Biblical narrative that lies at the heart of the Jewish experience. This is true for Christians in the West as well: the Holocaust and the Bible, interpreted within the context of the 20th century, have lead to an almost uncritical acceptance of the Jewish and Israeli narrative. This narrative has led to a politics that has favored Israel over the Palestinians to the point where during much of the last decades Palestinians have been invisible to most Jews and Christians or seen as terrorist threats long before the events of September 11th.

Israel has been supported throughout by a narrative that has the Holocaust at its center, and though this narrative is often seen as reductive and narrow, reflections on the Holocaust have great depth philosophically and theologically. Beginning in earnest in the mid-1960s, especially with the publication of Richard Rubenstein's *After Auschwitz* in 1966, the Holocaust became central to the Jewish discussion of Israel after Israel's victory in the 1967 Arab-Israeli War. Holocaust commentaries reached their zenith of reflection and power during the 1970s and 1980s, culminating in 1988 with Rabbi Irving Greenberg's essay "The Ethics of Jewish Power" as a response to the Palestinian uprising that began in 1987.[2]

There is much to say about what I have termed Holocaust Theology. Holocaust theologians ask deep questions about the possibility of belief about God after the Holocaust; they also take seriously the nature of power and how communities survive and flourish after catastrophe. Moreover, these theologians probe the material aspects of ethics and religiosity, bringing together community empowerment and a fragmented belief system as a religious obligation.

It is no secret that the Holocaust narrative, with its theological, political and ethical implications, has dominated Jewish consciousness for almost four decades. Its almost unqualified support for Israel as the primary response to Jewish suffering is also well known, as are the consequences for the Palestinian struggle. What is less known are the other understandings within the Jewish world that have suffered diminution and disappearance in the wake of what can only be called the tidal wave of Holocaust consciousness. Submerged are other possibilities and contradictions that, if sorted out, might create a parallel understanding of Jewish existence after the Holocaust, one that might bring us beyond the present impasse in which we find ourselves.

Martin Buber and Hannah Arendt are two Jewish philosophers/ ethicists who are interesting in this regard. Buber and Arendt were both European Jews who were forced to flee Nazi Germany in the 1930s, Buber ending up in Palestine and Arendt in America. Though Buber was intentionally Jewish, writing on Jewish topics as a committed Jew, and Arendt was Jewish by birth, writing on broad historical and philosophical themes that involved Jews but had a more universal bent, they both argued for a bi-nationalism in relation to Palestine, Jews and Arabs living together in a unified Palestine. Coming from somewhat different political and religious directions, they both opposed the creation of a Jewish state; still, they were both, again for somewhat different reasons, Zionists, homeland/cultural/spiritual Zionists rather than the political Zionism that triumphed in the creation of the state of Israel.[3]

Though Buber and Arendt are known as two of the most significant Jewish thinkers of the 20th century by Jews and non-Jews alike, their understandings of Palestine and bi-nationalism are relatively unknown in the Jewish community and beyond. With both, their arguments in relation to Zionism and politics, Jewishness and power, the Holocaust and the future of Jews and the world, are relatively unknown or simply dismissed as peripheral to their thought. In fact, just the opposite is the case; both in Buber and Arendt their Zionism and bi-nationalism are central to their thinking about politics and the world and the Jewish place in politics and the world. Far from being peripheral, Buber and Arendt cannot be understood apart from their thinking in this area.

Buber and Arendt have extended and complex arguments in this area of their thought; still it is possible to outline the central understandings of each and to see how their understandings lost out in the triumph of political Zionism and in the mainstream understandings of what it means to be Jewish in the world. My thesis is that the triumph of political Zionism is a reflection of the power of the state of Israel and post-Holocaust Jewish under-standings of the world Jews live and can survive within. Thus, there is a historical understanding of Buber and Arendt that is worth probing as well as understanding how this historical analysis might interrupt a future that seems to have no opposition or terminus. My reflections of Buber and Arendt are therefore geared to think about the future.

Buber was a Zionist because he believed that Palestine was the spiritual center of the Jewish people and that it had become obvious that Jews needed that center to renew their heritage and ethical strength. Zionism for Buber was pre-Holocaust, beginning long before the Nazis, and he also argued, almost from the beginning, with a Zionist program that saw the primary purpose of Jewish settlement in Palestine as a normalization of the Jewish condition in relation to the modern nation-state system. Buber's sense of Jewishness was far from this notion of normalization, a nation like

4

any other nation; just the opposite, Buber had an extraordinarily high sense of Jewish distinctiveness, chosenness if you will, that marked Jews in relation to the other nations. The Jewish return to the land of its origins was for Buber the re-rooting of this distinctiveness in its own soil without which the Diaspora branches would whither and might ultimately die.

These roots in the land were primarily spiritual and cultural; they also had a political dimension in the way that Buber envisioned a politics of communal self-governance that for Israel, the people, at least, was poised within an encounter with the deepest recesses of Jewish history and available to every Jewish generation. This politics was self-generated, with a communal focus that is related to Jewish spirituality and culture rather than the politics of the state, the state being for Buber a modern non-Jewish invention that prized a false universality and established a structure foreign to Jewish sensibilities.

In short, there was everything Jewish about a communal encounter in the Diaspora and in Palestine; nation-states, in Europe and elsewhere, had little if anything to say to Jews and Jewish history. For Buber, they were outer shells that had little to do with the thrust of Jewish history and the Jewish mission in the world. Israel, as a state, posed more or less the same straitjacket on Jewish aspirations. Indeed, such a state might be worse, posing as a surrogate, an idol, for what Jews needed to pursue as their destiny. That destiny, to be a Holy Nation, was found before the nation-state system, and had nothing to do with its structures of normalization, citizenship and power. Just the opposite, Buber argued that it was within a recognized but spiritually-oriented community that Jews could find their rootedness and therefore their mission again. The state, especially a Jewish one, had another trajectory.

Unlike Buber, Hannah Arendt was a Zionist for political reasons but which, on the surface at least, paradoxically led her, like Buber, to bi-nationalism. Buber was bi-nationalist because he realized, as Arendt did, that Arabs existed in the land and that peace with the Arab majority was crucial to Jewish settlement there. For Buber, peace with the Arab majority would allow the Jewish community to pursue its spiritual, cultural and educational re-rooting without taking on state structures that would divert Israel from its mission. Arendt, much more of a secular political thinker, and more influenced by the collapse of Europe and its Enlightenment sensibility during the Nazi era, found bi-nationalism as an example of new politics that was protective and depended on an interdependent empowerment that did not consume all the energies of the people.

Arendt, like Buber, also saw the Jewish people as being different but mostly from its minority and discriminated status. The question for Arendt was how the survivors of the Holocaust and Jews in the world could feel and be at home in the world after the Nazi terror and in the modern world. This could only happen with a politics that was genuine and open, connecting with others in building structures of governance that would be mutually beneficial and did not overpower the human.

Totality and its goals were already in full bloom in the world and at such a cost to the human. The Jewish community in Palestine could pioneer a different form of an integrated politics with Arabs in Palestine. This could also expand to become a regional federation. Thus, for Arendt, the entire Middle East could become an experiment in an alternative politics in the post-totalitarian era. Israel as a state, however, would embrace of totality in the region, dividing Jew from Arab in perpetuity, and therefore creating a state structure that would of necessity be on a permanent war footing. This permanent war footing would dampen and ultimately extinguish debate and intellectual development in the Jewish world that might have, with others, charted a new direction in a world badly in need of alternative examples of embodied politics.

There is much more to say about Buber and Arendt in their different approaches to the same conclusion. Both Buber and Arendt came to their bi-nationalism through an understanding of the peculiar Jewish situation in the world. For both, Jews were distinctive yet small in number; Jews could testify to a world beyond violence partly because of this. Both saw only danger in the attempt to normalize the Jewish situation through statehood. Statehood would

6

destroy everything that the bi-nationalism could salvage and present to the Jewish world and others as a positive model in the post-World War II era. Arendt was more influenced than Buber by the experience of Nazism, though both had to respond to the rising number of Jews in Palestine caused by the Nazi onslaught and the increasing clamor, because of the situation, for a Jewish state in Palestine. The consequences of the establishment of a Jewish state, especially the cleansing of large numbers of Palestinians from the territory that would become Israel, foretold for both disasters ahead.

Reading Buber's and Arendt's warnings of that time show how aware they were of the consequences of a politics of dispossession and power enshrined in an emerging state. These consequences included the failure of the Jewish ethical tradition, the quashing of internal dissent and the positing of an exclusive right to narrate a univocal understanding of history, especially a reification of Jew-hatred. In sum, the consequences of statehood would be a disaster for Jews and Arabs. And the world.

Buber and Arendt came from different angles of vision to the same conclusion. They also shared certain prejudices inherent in their formative years as Jews and Europeans in the 20ᵗʰ century. These prejudices were not overcome by their trenchant and laudable analysis of what would befall the Middle East if a Jewish state was established and then pursued as an end unto itself. In general, the prejudice was both Jewish and European: Jewish in the sense that both held a certain sense of chosenness about Jews in general, though argued on quite different grounds, and a sense of Western superiority to the East, shared in large part by Jews and non-Jews in Europe.

The Jewish sense of specialness, Biblically and then transferred to intellectual capabilities in Enlightenment Europe, is well known. Both Buber and Arendt shared aspects of these understandings. Though a sense of specialness can be found in most traditions and communities, the task is to direct this understanding to the good of the community and others. In large part Buber and Arendt attempted to do this. Yet, perhaps inevitably, specialness morphs into superiority; Buber's and Arendt's arguments are filled with these notions of superiority toward the Arabs of Palestine and the region. Both see the Arabs as backward and in need of uplift. Jews can be useful in that arena and that, in part, can be seen as an argument, if not justification, for the settling of a growing number of European Jews in Palestine.

The argument for European civilization and for Jews as the spearhead of that civilization might seem strange in the context of the Nazi debacle at the very heart of European "civilization", the primary victims of which were the Jews of Europe. However, this simply goes to show how deep this sense of European superiority was at the time. Of course, this superiority claim is endemic to the entire Jewish enterprise in Palestine, the Jewish claims, to be sure, but also the purposeful construction of a Western style economy and culture in the land with Arab culture being seen as foreign and as a hindrance of the development of civilization in the area.

Here we begin to explore the underbelly of Jewish analysis with regard to Palestine, then Israel, coloring the entire enterprise of statehood and the continuing debate within the Jewish community about the direction of the Jewish state. In essence, the sense of Jewish specialness and superiority of the West, coupled with the Holocaust narrative that overwhelmed Buber's and Arendt's bi-nationalism, has allowed Israel the support it needs to pursue then and now a policy of ethnic cleansing and occupation without stating either as policies and with the possibility of denying both as a matter of accepted discourse within the Jewish community and in the West.

When the brakes on Jewish empowerment in Palestine, then Israel, are released, the sense of specialness and superiority take on a life of their own. The question then is how all of this might have played out if Jewish particularity had not been so strong and, of course, if the Nazis had not risen to power. These historical questions are perhaps unanswerable. However, the questions remain important for the future: Is there a way to negotiate the Jewish narrative that does not limit Palestinian aspirations and their own sense of destiny? Or does the Jewish narrative have to be abandoned altogether if peace and justice between Israel/Palestine is to come into being?

Emmanuel Levinas was also born in Europe, in Kaunas, Lithuania, lived in France before the Nazi period and survived there during and after the Nazi years. With Buber and Arendt, Levinas is also one of the most significant Jewish philosophers of the 20th century. Unlike Buber and Arendt, who both wrote extensively about Palestine and then Israel in direct political terms, arguing for certain political structures of the community and against others, Levinas circles these issues, preferring to comment, for the most, indirectly about the emergence and well being of the state of Israel.

Levinas, ostensibly a European philosopher, is Judeo-centric. Or rather it is more accurate to say that there are two sides of Levinas, the first being strictly European and arguing his philosophy in those terms, the second being strictly Jewish; it is here that he argues the question of politics and Israel for Jews within a Judaic framework. One might argue that Levinas brings together, in his unique way, the sides that Buber and Arendt argue singularly. If both Buber and Arendt pioneered Jewish influence on philosophy during the 1960s and 1970s, it can be argued that Levinas does the same in the 1990s and beyond. It is difficult to exaggerate Levinas' influence in academic circles today; yet his Jewish writings and where they lead on the question of Israel are hardly known and rarely analyzed. Levinas shares the same fate as Buber and Arendt on questions that were of great importance to them.[4]

Like Buber and Arendt, it is impossible to capture Levinas' thought in a few paragraphs or in a few books for that matter. Nonetheless, it is important to begin to analyze Levinas in this way as it yields further questions about how Jews think about Israel, then and now. It may also yield further insight into the path that needs to be pursued in the present.

Levinas is ambivalent about the emergence of a Jewish state. Ambivalent, yes, but also reluctant to discuss it fully or directly. The Holocaust is uppermost in his mind, Jews having just suffered mass death. Yet also and perhaps with priority, the Jews is a community with a mission before and beyond the state; the special language of the Judaic is found in sacred texts rather than in territory. Jews guard these texts, the Torah and the Talmud, and it is here that Jews find their special destiny. And contribute to the world. Nation-states come and go. Moreover they use violence to survive. Shall Israel, the people, take on the violence of the world?

Israel, the state, has taken on the violence of the world; Levinas is ambivalent. On the one hand, Israel, the people, cannot help but be affected by the state; on the other hand, who among the nations can or should lecture Israel, the people and the state, about violence? After all, Israel must survive in the world to accomplish its mission. It was that very danger to Israel's existence that made Israel, the state, necessary.

The issue is complex, and Levinas goes back and forth on this matter. Levinas warns Israel, the people and state, of what is befalling them. He also warns the world to back off; the world, having violated Israel for so long, has no moral lessons to communicate. But there is another more disturbing understanding that can also be found in Levinas. That is the neighbor, so important to his philosophy, as the commanding voice that the self is responsible to and for, is only Jewish. Or primarily so. But certainly not "Afro-Asiatic", Levinas' encompassing term for the Third World, which in broad strokes includes Arabs and Palestinians.

For Levinas, the Third World is teeming with the uncivilized, sometimes referred to as hordes, waiting to invade the civilized West. Again we find the irony of Jews seeing the West as civilized and the East as not; Levinas does vacillate, catching himself, and sometimes seeing Islam as part of the civilized world, though not primarily or usually. In general, however, Levinas is Euro-centric and identifies Jews within that framework. Jewish distinctiveness comes within the European framework; rarely in Levinas' work are Jews seen within global humanity.[5]

Israel, the state, then, is seen within the context of Europe. The reason for its being is Europe; also its protection. Though inhabiting the land of the Bible, for Levinas, Israel is located in an uncomfortable neighborhood. Its only protection is Europe and a European-oriented state. Mostly unsaid but lurking in the background, is Israel's fight with the pagan world, now begun again in the Middle East. Salvation comes from Europe, the same place that damned the Jews during Levinas' lifetime.

There is much more to be said about the relation of Jews, Judaism and Israel in all three philosophers I have been exploring; yet the broad outlines of the problematic can be seen, especially when we factor in the explosion of Holocaust consciousness and theology that has made all but invisible the nuances in these great—but also limited—Jewish philosophers.

The question remains: Are there aspects of thought within Holocaust theology, Martin Buber, Hannah Arendt and Emmanuel Levinas that can help move the question of Israel/Palestine forward? We are, at this moment, in the latest point possible, politically and ethically. The damage done, with Israel controlling, seeming indefinitely, millions of Palestinians within the expanded state of Israel now stretching from Tel Aviv to the Jordan River, the Wall almost complete and with the war in Lebanon just fought and other wars on the horizon. Is there a way to reverse course, bring Israel back to a sane and just foreign policy and restore Palestinians to land and justice? The situation being what it is, is there time left to think philosophically about Israel/Palestine?

The Jewish narrative that has supported Israel throughout its existence is comprised of a variety of elements that are shared by most Jewish commentators, theologians and philosophers. The first is the unique aspect of the Judaic, variously described and grounded, but shared across the spectrum of Jewish reflection. Coupled with this sense of uniqueness is the shared horror at the Holocaust and the sense that the Holocaust is a watershed event in the history of the Jewish people and the world. Approached from a variety of angles, the Holocaust either demands or accelerates the Jewish need for a place in Palestine, then Israel.

The bi-nationalism of Buber and Arendt seems unfortunate or safe in the past, depending on one's point of view. Also—unfortunate or

11

safe—Levinas' conflicted sense of the state as needed and as a threat to Jewish ethics, seems to be past. Again this depends on the point of view of the observer; from another perspective bi-nationalism and ambivalence regarding the state of Israel might be a way of raising question about the future of Israel and the Palestinians. The past is past, and certainly we have moved so far beyond these initial questionings that a call for retreat or retrospective grumbling seems futile. The question of the future is on our doorstep; it is the only relevant question.

The hesitations in these Jewish philosophers also provide a stumbling block that may be key in addressing the possibility, or impossibility, of creating a future different than the past. This has to do with the agreement found among them but also the widely shared understanding in the contemporary Jewish world that the "Arabs" cannot be trusted and that they represent the modern extension of the anti-Semitic past. The question of Arabs and anti-Semitism is crucial here, all having to do with the fear of the Orient and, sad to say, a racism toward Middle Eastern peoples.

Within this context, Buber, Arendt and Levinas, seem backward looking, carrying a Western sensibility toward the East and Arabs that is difficult to justify or explain; it can only be seen as a deeply ingrained prejudice. Add to this the increased sense of distrust by Jews in the wake of the events of September 11th, a new emphasis on Islam as a retrograde force in the world, then the circle of Jewish hesitancy in relation to the Middle East is closed. Islam is not emphasized in any of these Jewish philosophers I have discussed; nor did it play a role in the origins and power of Holocaust Theology. It does, however, represent an extension of these understandings. It makes it even more difficult to suggest alternative possibilities for the state of Israel from an internal Jewish perspective.

What happens when even the internal brakes within an ethical and philosophical religious system are overcome by its own ambivalence and the circumstances of state power? Though in this case a specifically Jewish experience, this problem is no doubt applicable to other systems of thought in relation to the communities and nation-state systems others live within. What are the lessons Jews need to learn, and others as well, in this uneven competition between ethical/ philosophical reflections and state power?

At least in the Jewish case, the situation of world Jewry for the last two thousand years did not prepare itself either for the trauma of the Holocaust or for the assumption of state power. The warnings of all three philosophers in this regard went unheeded and their predictions of the consequences of state power have all come true. And more. The sense that, once assumed, state power would propel Jews into an assimilation to violence and uniformity of thought has been achieved in a way approaching totality. Their predictions that this assimilation to power and the state would marginalize and even criminalize dissent have also come to fruition. However, what none of these philosophers predicted in terms of the longevity of dissent has also come to pass; the continuation and deepening of conscience among some Jews, in short the emergence of Jews of Conscience within Israel and the Diaspora.

Jews of Conscience pick up on aspects of all three philosophers we have analyzed as well as aspects of Holocaust Theology; they carry these understandings into the 21st century with the situation of Israel/Palestine as it is now. Buber's and Arendt's bi-nationalism for example; seeing that the two state solution, two real states with Palestinians controlling the West Bank, East Jerusalem and Gaza as an integral unit, as past. Jews of Conscience begin to think through how the two peoples can live together in one state within the context of a transformed relationship. Whereas, Buber and Arendt were tying to keep Palestine undivided and therefore avoid boundaries that would limit the flourishing of Jews and Palestinians, Jews of Conscience are interested in seeing how the divisions created in 1948 and extended ever since can be crossed and healed. Could the trauma of the Holocaust and the displacement of the Palestinians be healed through a revived sense of the bi-nationalism within the state, once called Palestine, now called Israel?

Israel, the people, through Israel, the state, has been using the state to their own advantage: Has there been such a thorough assimilation

13

to the violence of the world that there is no way back? Of course, there is never a way back; the question revolves around alternatives for the future. Can Jews of Conscience find a way which allows a secure life for Jews and Palestinians in the land, one that features justice and reconciliation, equality and eventual forgiveness, and thus in the coming years promote a revolutionary justice and forgiveness? The first item on the agenda is ending the cycle of violence and atrocity; the second is the meeting of Jews and Palestinians in the broken middle of Jerusalem where a different future can be charted.

To begin again, the prophetic, the indigenous spirituality of Israel, the people—a formulation indebted to Martin Buber—must be re-embraced. Buber wrote of this explicitly; he applied aspects of that prophetic sensibility to bi-nationalism. Still he fell short as his Judeo-centric and Western prejudice limited his ability to follow this line of thought to the end. Levinas was split on the prophetic, writing beautifully and compellingly on the subject; this was tempered by his reliance on the Rabbinic as the essence of Judaism. Rabbinic Judaism, honed in a time when Jews were outside the land and, for the most part, existing as minorities in unstable majority situations, subverted the prophetic with textual reasoning and legal rulings.

Jews of Conscience must re-embrace the prophetic without Judeo-centric superiority and Rabbinic sensibilities. This is impossible without the framework of Jewish identity today. Thus, exile from mainstream Judaism is certain, but a deeper question is raised as to whether Israel, the state, can be supported at all within these prophetic understandings. If such a state can be supported, will there come a time when it needs to be abandoned, that is, a time when the decision is made that the violence taken on is of Israel's history and will remain as such? Such a time may come and sooner than expected. Will that mean that Israel, the people, has also taken on that violence as constitutive of its being, therefore prompting Jews of Conscience to renounce not only Israel, the state, but also Israel, the people?

The questions here are many. The situation worsens daily, and any lull in the process of decline buys time for Israel; peace processes actually facilitate a further deterioration of the Palestinian situation. Jews of Conscience within Israel are caught within a state that is deaf to their concerns. Their ethical concerns are overpowered by state power. Jews in the Diaspora continue to speak in the American and European context but, alas, they too are overpowered by the religious and political discourse that champions Israel at the detriment of the Palestinians.

Though over time there has been some modification of the Israel bias in the American media and political spectrum, September 11th and the policies of the Bush administration have, of course, "corrected" any suspected drift toward Palestinians. The response to the recent book of former President, Jimmy Carter, *Palestine: Peace Not Apartheid* is a case in point. Released just weeks after the election victory of the Democrats in November 2006, the newly empowered Democratic Senate and House leadership distanced themselves from Carter in no uncertain terms. They feared reprisals from their funding and voting bloc as well as losses in the political narrative that might catapult them to a further and decisive victory in 2008.[6]

The road ahead is unknown; a positive resolution of the Israeli-Palestinian conflict is unlikely in the near future. Surely, there are many reasons for this present and future failure. One of them is the Jewish narrative, even as represented by great Jewish philosophers like Buber, Arendt and Levinas. Though they show us a way to at least doubt the Holocaust and state narrative in place, their own Judeo-centric and prejudicial sensibilities help limit our movement toward a just resolution of the decades old conflict. The question remains as to whether Jews of Conscience can move with and beyond Buber, Arendt and Levinas or whether Jews are now in a situation where there is no exit from the trajectory that is obvious.

Notes

1. The third edition is expanded and with new material. See *Toward a Jewish Theology of Liberation: The Challenge of the 21st Century* (Waco, Texas: Baylor University Press, 2004).

2. I trace the themes of Holocaust Theology in ibid. 15–74.

3. Most of the material I use on Martin Buber and Hannah Arendt and their bi-nationalism can be found in *A Land of Two Peoples: Martin Buber on Jews and Arabs*, ed. Paul Mendes-Flohr (New York: Oxford University Press, 1983) and *Hannah Arendt: The Jew as Pariah*, ed. Ron Feldman (New York: Grove Press, 1978). See also a new and enlarged edition of this book, *Hannah Arendt: The Jewish Writings*, ed. Jerome Kohn and Ron Feldman (New York: Schocken Books, 2007).

4. For an extended and fascinating analysis of Levinas on the political dimensions of Israel see Howard Caygill, *Levinas and the Political* (London: Routledge, 2002): 159–198.

5. Ibid. 182–185.

6. Jimmy Carter, *Palestine: Peace Not Apartheid* (New York: Simon and Shuster, 2006).

DIALOGUE AMONG CIVILIZATIONS AFTER 9/11
A Jewish Vision of Solidarity for a
Post-September 11ᵗʰ World*

The literature describing the meaning of the September 11ᵗʰ world is so voluminous that it is difficult for any one person to read, let alone digest it all. Though this literature continues to proliferate, as a response to a historical event its cutting-edge quality has reached its limit. Perhaps this is because we are entering a post-September 11ᵗʰ period. Though defining in the present decade, September 11ᵗʰ is receding in its distinctiveness. September 11ᵗʰ should now be seen as an intensification of historical trends rather than an incisive break with the past.[1]

As often is the case, the reactions after a historical event—characterized as such—are written under the duress and excitement of the moment. Something out of the ordinary has happened to which we must pay attention. Yet that "after" moment ultimately settles into a historical sequence. The event, ultimately seen as formative, with time and reflection recedes in importance. Or the event's importance takes its place within a broader history. Formative events are by their nature defining, yet in the end they redefine a historical journey, emphasizing certain particulars and distancing others.

We should now see September 11ᵗʰ in this light from whatever vantage point it is viewed. Obviously the American context is only one place to view this event; Afghanistan and Iraq are other contexts from which to view September 11ᵗʰ. If we factor in Pakistan the aftershocks of September 11ᵗʰ are expanded in geography, culture and religion. Even this expansion is limiting. If we take into account the Israeli-Palestinian conflict, global movements of trade and currency and other "security" liaisons around the world, September 11ᵗʰ ceases to be an American or regional event. Trying to

---

* 2008 Global Forum on Civilization and Peace, Academy of Korean Studies Republic of Korea, May 27–29, 2008.

17

place September 11th in perspective in no way seeks to minimize the disastrous policies implemented in its wake.

Though often analyzed within the broader rubric of the clash of civilizations, September 11th is better seen within the intensification of global inequalities, imperial ambitions and the struggles of power elites for control of domestic politics and wealth. Of course, all of these are continuing processes as old as human history. September 11th has produced winners and losers as other events in history have, with, as often is the case in history, struggles still to be decided.

In Pakistan for example, the recent assassination of Benazir Bhutto exemplifies the continuing effects of September 11th. Pakistan has a rich and difficult political history where political rivals, including Bhutto's father, pay the ultimate price. So political assassination in Pakistani politics is nothing new. Pakistan's relationship with the United States also has a complex history that predates September 11th. This means that the present American support for the Musharraf government and its aid to Pakistan as a bulwark against terrorism is a continuation of past policies.[2]

So too, the Israeli-Palestinian crisis. Existing now for more than sixty years, September 11th gave Israel a further green light to crush the Palestinian uprising that began in 2000 as well as allow it to consolidate its hold on Jerusalem, give Israel more latitude to expand its territory in the West Bank and increase the number of settlements and settlers in the occupied territories. In the case of Israel and the Palestinians, the Israelis, posing as a historic front line against Arab and Third World assaults on the West, gained a new and welcome lease on life.

For some years, critical analysis of Israeli policies against Palestinians chipped away at the mythology of Israel's innocence and, at least in the West, was diminishing the demonization of the Palestinian cause. While not reversing this analytical trend, September 11th kept new understandings from entering the political arena. It allowed Israel to use the September 11th umbrella to further its historic policies of creating facts on the ground that would become the new point of departure for the peace process. This

18

meant that the expansion and settlements created after September 11th were added to the expansion and settlements of previous decades. As usual international events and alliances provided Israel ideological space to accomplish the practical details of building a Jewish state that has nothing to do with events outside its sphere of influence.[3]

In the Israeli-Palestinian crisis and in so many other ways, then, September 11th has functioned as a green light for policies and ambitions already in view; over the last years it has become a cover for the continuation and intensification of these policies. In the post-September 11th period it is important to lift the cover and see the policies being pursued in various parts of the world for what they had been and for what they are. Simply put, the aftereffects of September 11th are in need of critical evaluation. Thus the question remains whether speaking of September 11th as a world changing, exceptional occurrence serves us well or itself becomes a launching point for critical thought that gives over too much to the powers that this event, at least as it has been interpreted, has served well.

So too, the clash of civilizations approach, developed before the September 11th event, but gaining even wider currency since then. The idea that distinct civilizations formed around discrete events and ideological/religious underpinnings—one's that are historically and inherently in conflict—needs demystifying as well. In the September 11th rhetoric, Islamic civilization is distinct and at war with Christian civilization or, altered for the pluralism of the West, Judeo-Christian civilization, and recent events simply bring this war to the forefront. This war, eternal as it is immediate, was "forgotten" by the liberalizing West in its rush to embrace pluralism and secularism. In this view, pluralism and secularism, indeed the entire liberal and universal project of the West, is exposed as shallow and naïve. Whatever one can say about the "goodness" of this project, it is distinctly Western and under assault by other civilizations who, though they may adopt a Western veneer, are profoundly Other in their primal sensibilities.

The September 11th worldview sees Western values, now distinctly American, as under a global assault. It is America's responsibility to

19

uphold, guard and disseminate these ideas within a hostile world. If, indeed, America fulfills its historic destiny as the promulgator, guardian, and upholder of the values that were born and bred within the West and in the bosom of Judeo-Christian civilization, then it is possible to change civilizations hostile to these ideas from within. At least this is the debate: whether or not these other civilizations can be changed—that is whether their hostility is simply a form of ignorance and backwardness which means that America's destiny is to change the world through the spread of democracy, liberty and Christianity—or whether these civilizations are unchangeable which means that America should withdraw to a Fortress America so that at least America can preserve the last light in an increasingly dark world.

On the Jewish take on September 11th there are three perspectives that flow from the divisions within the Jewish world. After a brief discussion of the divisions within Israel, I will concentrate on the divisions within the Jewish community in America.

Within the governing circles of Israel, September 11th gave a green light for then Prime Minister Ariel Sharon to continue his policies of expansionism and settlement in Jerusalem and the West Bank. At the same time, he was able to evict the Jewish settlers of Gaza while working with Egypt to seal Gaza's borders. These borders are with Israel, Egypt, and the West Bank Palestinians. By withdrawing settlers from Gaza, Sharon effectively encircled Gaza and further diminished the connections between the now three remnant Palestinian populations within the effective control of Israel: the Palestinians within Israel (1.3 million); the Palestinians within Jerusalem and the West Bank (2.5 million); the Palestinians in Gaza (1.4 million).[4]

Dissenting circles within Israel have increased and diminished over the years. After September 11th a further diminishment of dissent occurred, at least as embodied in the two-state solution Israeli peace camp. With the continual erosion of support and land for such a solution and with the rise of Hamas and a more active military campaign waged by the Palestinians and then later by Hezbollah in the 2006 Lebanon war, many Jews on the Left left the Left.

Whether in fact they were ever serious about recognizing the political rights of Palestinians to a real, contiguous and viable state with East Jerusalem as its capital is a question.

Whatever their deeper objectives, in the aftermath of September 11th, the Israeli peace movement was in shambles. What remained, and this is intriguing, is a series of smaller, more serious and incisive groups of Israelis that recognized what Israel had done to the Palestinians in the creation of Israel and its connection to contemporary policies of the Israeli state. This was summarized by the fascinating book by a group of Israeli architects who linked the dislocation of Palestinians and the Jewish settlements that took their land and their place with the creation of the state of Israel. The process was also named by such prominent Israeli political and academic figures as Meron Benvenisti and Ilan Pappe as ethnic cleansing.[5]

The post-September 11th American Jewish scene is divided as it was before between the Constantinian Jewish establishment, Progressive Jews and Jews of Conscience. These are obvious designations, with the Constantinian Jewish establishment being comprised of politically connected Jews, the Jewish religious establishment and Jewish intellectuals in the academy and media. Progressive Jews are those in the religious and intellectual spheres who argue for a more even-handed approach to the issues of power, especially in the Israel-Palestine realm, but who seek, if their dissent is accepted, to become the next Jewish establishment. Jews of Conscience see the difficulty in aligning with power and the refusal to probe the deeper dimensions of Israel's history then and now as a fault line that forces their exile from the Constantinian and Progressive Jewish communities.

Alone among these segments of the Jewish community and located both in America and Israel, Jews of Conscience are probing deeper as they journey into the post-September 11th world. In recognizing continuity between the pre-September 11th and the September 11th world, Jews of Conscience probe a series of relations and scenarios that might break this assumed discontinuity that masks a continuity that is dangerous and unproductive. Among the issues that Jews of

Conscience seek to analyze is how Jewish power is being used in the United States and Israel and what can be done to break down the barriers between people of conscience around the world. Instead of a clash of civilizations, Jews of Conscience search for a solidarity that exists among those in every part of the globe and within every religion and culture in the support of human and political rights that are personal and communal. In so doing, Jews of Conscience both support particularity and the universality that crosses geographic, political, cultural and religious borders.[6]

If the September 11th worldview is one of polarities, good versus evil, Jews of Conscience understand the world of difference as a possible path of solidarity when the distinctives of culture, politics and religion are seen from another angle of vision in a post-September 11th framework. In the September 11th good versus evil scenario, the mainstream of the "good", usually associated with power and a collective sense of innocence, is aligned against the mainstream of the "bad", usually associated with power and the underdevelopment of the misguided. In the American schema, American democracy and Christianity are pitted against Third World authoritarian regimes and Islam. In this simplified analysis of the world, links with the good can be salvaged and supported so that parts of Islam insofar as they become Westernized and Americanized can be salvaged. At the same time, the use of the bad by the good to punish others who are even worse is justified until the situation changes. A case in point is Saddam Hussein, seen by America as a useful ally at one point, who later became a dangerous enemy. Jews and Judaism once classified as heretical and dangerous are now an integral ally of American power.

The shifting boundaries of these two cases, Saddam Hussein's Iraq and Jews in the West, among many others, demonstrate that the clash of civilizations hides a power politics and opportunism of nations, communities and individuals. Civilization, however that is defined, is like a movable goal post and a removable one at that. At any moment a course of action and ideas can be reversed and transcended when other interests are at stake. If this is true among the powerful, can it also be true among those who cross lines for the sake of the disenfranchised and marginal? Instead of civilizations at war or at peace, perhaps it is better to think of alliances within and across political, cultural and religious boundaries that serve certain interests.

For Jews of Conscience this is particularly important as they wage a struggle within the Jewish community for Jewish ethics. Jews of Conscience understand the Jewish ethical challenge as both particular to its own history and universal in relation to bonding with others for justice and peace. The inward turning of the Jewish community after the Holocaust and with the formation of the state of Israel has meant a process of normalization in the world. In short this means that Jews empowered are now participating in the same policies that once caused our exclusion and suffering. This shift in Jewish behavior comports with the changed context of Jewish life. But since the indigenous of Jewish history remains the prophetic, there are some Jews who embrace that prophetic heritage in an age where Jewish power seeks to discipline, dismiss and even destroy. Jews of Conscience have no alternative but to take their battle within and outside of their communal boundaries.

In doing so Jews are involved with people of conscience within the Jewish community and in other communities. This includes such diverse groups as Palestinians of good will, Christians in America who are disaffected with American empire, Third World peoples who are embracing Liberation Theology and Muslims of conscience around the world. These minorities who often represent "civilizations" are often also disaffected with the policies and attitudes of the mainstream community they were born and raised in. The same goes when their political, cultural and religious leaders use the broad arc of civilizational politics to create and maintain their power. If Jews of Conscience are in exile, aren't there many others throughout the world who can also claim this exile status in the post-September 11th world?

Increasingly, Jews, Christians and Muslims of Conscience are in exile from the state power they live within and from the global economic order that prevails. When they are rallied within their religious communities, they also find themselves out of step; often they find themselves closer to one another in different communities in different geographic locales. Thus, a sense of exile is complimented by a sense of belonging.

This "belonging" might be what I call a broader tradition of faith and struggle. This tradition is expansive, crossing boundaries and borders; like any tradition it has broad shared understandings and a history, even if that history is only being recognized here and now. That this tradition is unnamed as yet doesn't preclude it from existing.

The question of naming has been and continues to be fraught with a variety of questions including loyalty to a named history and fear of the unknown naming. If as a Jew, I belong to a community that has Muslims and Christians; does this make me cease to be Jewish? If I feel closer to an agnostic or even an atheist in the struggle for justice, does this compromise my belief in God? If as a Jew, I am in solidarity with the aspirations of the Palestinian people, does this make the accusations of treason made against me seem plausible even sometimes to myself?[7]

The questions of people of conscience, wherever they are, probe the roots of our situation and refuse surface answers. Responses and excuses offered by political and religious authorities are rejected. Rejecting the surface answers offered as if they were ordained, people of conscience are forced to cross borders and boundaries for different ways of asking questions and for support they rarely find where they are. Thus Jews can learn from Muslims and Muslims from Jews. Certain aspects of another's culture or religion might help elucidate what the authorities cover up within one's own community. Sometimes the help needed is right here where we come from; it has disappeared from sight. Other times the help needed is truly missing from our backgrounds. Crossing boundaries and borders can therefore help illumine our home turf as well as help us evolve beyond what has been present. In the process what has been perceived as the Other becomes closer; the stranger becomes neighbor. On the other side, as the Other becomes neighbor, neighbor might perceive you as becoming Other.

24

That latter perception might be correct, at least partially. If the broader tradition of faith is my tradition, then it is also my community. Since that community is for the most part far away physically and mostly exists in history, a sense of being foreign— from both sides—is appropriate. This foreignness is alienation from what is; it is embracing a future that is not yet, yet one that has existed and exists now.

The duality of embracing a community that is invisible and present defines a person of conscience since everything inherited and proposed as embodied values in the world is under scrutiny. That is the borders and boundaries of the world we inherited and the one that is questioned and traversed. The person of conscience is at home only in the dynamic of going under and out from what has been and is—as defined as normative. The normative itself is too little and too late. It has an answer to the why of every injustice and violence as it continues to press down on those who are vulnerable and outside.

Striving toward a post-September 11th understanding of the world, does that mean exile is inevitable? Does exile immobilize us in acting in relation to what the persons of conscience understand? Does the exile have a responsibility to maintain his or her cover and stay where they come from for politically efficacious reasons if for none other? If their cover is exposed and they are thrown out, should they fight their way back to respectability within the community they do and do not belong to? Is it better to have one foot in and one foot out of one's community, rather than being only out? Is out only out or is out in the new community that might one day be organized as a force in the world? Or does that force—might we call it a remnant force—have its own power beyond what is organized and seen according to the political and religious rules in play?

By adopting a post-September 11th worldview we enter a different space where people of all cultures and faiths are called to analyze what is around and beneath the present economic, political and military global order. Since those who support this order bond across boundaries and borders, shouldn't those who seek another way of life also bond in the same way? This necessitates a violation of various patterns of thought and identification, including identity orthodoxies and civilizational constructs that keep our field of vision restricted and often immobilized.

On the Jewish side, the challenge is to refuse the definition of communal loyalty as sufficient for our Jewishness, at the same time, investigating alternative patterns of Jewish identification as we practice solidarity with others. Going out to others means the refusal to stop at the water's edge even when assaulted by the epithet of self-hating Jew and the charge of treason.

But isn't this the same charge leveled in other religious, ethnic and national communities, when the future is seen in a way that the powers that be don't recognize as their own trajectory? In the gathering of exiles into a New Diaspora community perhaps the assault of these charges can be minimized in their impact. Drawing a new boundary and border can help protect, mobilize and invigorate the alternatives that are desperately needed in a post-September 11th world.

Notes

1. For one of my earlier articles on September 11th contained in a book of essays on this subject see "After September 11th: The Struggle to Redefine Jewish Identity," in *9/11 and the American Empire: Christians, Jews and Muslims Speak Out*, ed. Kevin Barrett, John Cobb and Sandra Lubarsky (North Hampton, MA: Olive Branch Press, 2007): 101–118.

2. On the ability of September 11th to cloud perceptions, the case of Benazir Bhutto in the wake of her assassination is telling. Seen by many Americans as a saint because of her promise to pursue terrorists and restore democracy in Pakistan as a bastion against Al Qaeda and the Taliban her past has been conveniently forgotten. For a take on this legacy see William Dalrymple, "Bhutto's Deadly Legacy," *New York Times*, January 4, 2008.

3. This cover included the reinvigoration of the use of anti-Semitism after September 11th as a reason to oppose political opposition to the continuing expansion of the Israeli state. For this argumentation see Abraham Foxman, *Never Again?: The Threat of the New Anti-Semitism* (San Francisco: HarperSanFrancisco, 2003).

4. On Sharon and the continuity of his vision see Baruch Kimmerling, *Politicide: The Real Legacy of Ariel Sharon* (London: Verso, 2006).

5. On the ethnic cleansing of Palestinians see Meron Benvenisti, *Sacred Landscape: The Buried History of the Holy Land Since 1948* (Berkeley: University of

California Press, 2000) and Ilan Pappe, *The Ethnic Cleansing of Palestine* (Oxford: One World, 2006).

6. For an extended analysis of Jews of Conscience see my latest work including third edition of *Toward a Jewish Theology of Liberation: The Challenge of the 21st Century* (Waco: Baylor University Press, 2004); *Reading the Torah Out Loud: A Journey of Lament and Hope* (Minneapolis: Fortress, 2007) and forthcoming *Judaism Does Not Equal Israel* (New York: New Directions, 2009).

7. For the religious questions that confront the exilic community of our time see my *Practicing Exile: The Journey of an American Jew* (Minneapolis: Fortress, 2002).

IF THE OCCUPATION IS PERMANENT, IS AN ETHICAL JEWISH FUTURE POSSIBLE?

*JEWS OF CONSCIENCE FACE THE FORBIDDING JEWISH FUTURE**

FOR THE LAST WEEK, I have been teaching and touring in the Old City of Jerusalem. Much has changed in the forty plus years since I first arrived in Jerusalem. It was October, 1973, six years after the 1967 Arab-Israeli war; the 1973 war began while I was here. In the ensuing years, I traveled to Jerusalem many times and written many words that emerged from my experiences in Israel-Palestine. During these years I have pursued a vision that came to me early on—that the future of the Jewish people is bound up with the fate of Palestine and Palestinians. On this, the 30th anniversary of my book, *Toward a Jewish Theology of Liberation*, I offer the following meditation on where we have arrived and where we are heading, Jews and Palestinians together.

Thirty years ago, in Jerusalem, at the Shalom Hartman Institute and the Tantur Ecumenical Institute, and in my book *Toward a Jewish Theology of Liberation*, I raised an unprecedented challenge to Jewish theologians, Jews interested in spirituality broadly speaking and Jewish seekers of justice from any perspective, whether articulated Jewishly or not: What does it mean, after the Holocaust, for empowered Jews in America, for empowered Jews in the state of

---

*. A lecture sponsored by the Tantur Ecumenical Institute and the Jerusalem Global Gateway of the University of Notre Dame, Jerusalem, Israel-Palestine, October 24, 2017.

Israel, for empowered Jews in the United Kingdom, in Argentina and wherever Jews live, to come into solidarity with the Palestinian people in their struggle to be free in their own homeland? It has been many years, truly a lifetime it seems, and the answer has not arrived. Now I ask a second, related challenge, thirty years later, again in Jerusalem, at Tantur and now at the Jerusalem School of Theology where I am teaching these weeks, to Jewish theologians, Jews interested in spirituality broadly speaking and to Jewish seekers of justice from any perspective, articulated Jewishly or not: What does it mean after the Holocaust *and* after Israel, meaning by that after what Israel has done and is doing to the Palestinian people, for empowered Jews in America, for empowered Jews in the state of Israel and wherever empowered Jews live around the world, to understand that the occupation of Palestinians and Palestine is permanent and that, therefore the possibility of an ethical Jewish future is foreclosed?[1]

I will return to the challenge of solidarity and a permanent occupation in a moment. First, though, a rehearsal of what has occurred between the time I spoke in Jerusalem thirty years ago and this evening, again in Jerusalem, as I speak. There are many, many details and more than a few seminal events to cite, yet the overall picture is our focus. Simply put, through hook and crook, the state of Israel has successfully pursued a well-defined, if only partially articulated, series of military, political and economic policies to extend Israel's reach into Palestine and consistently diminish Palestinian politics, culture and religion.

Thirty years ago the occupation of Palestine and Palestinians may have already been permanent. Today, no analyst anywhere worth listening to can deny the permanence of Israel's occupation. Every plan put forward by Israel, by the Palestinians and by the international community - in substance if not in rhetoric - recognizes Israel's superior power and geographic expansion as permanent. Every plan put forward by Israel, the Palestinians and by the international community - in substance if not in rhetoric - proposes only a limited autonomy for Palestinians, an autonomy further constrained by military forces from various countries and entities that includes, among others, the American and Israeli military. There is no serious political or military force in the world that proposes an end to Israel's occupation. And further, during these thirty years a startling increase in overt strategic military cooperation with Israel has occurred within the Arab world. In short, Israel has become a permanent occupier of Palestine and a strategic asset of major players in the Arab world.

There is no need to define permanent as duration, as forever. Or to speculate on scenarios as to how the permanent occupation of Palestine and Palestinians can be reversed. History is open; unforeseen events occur. The change agent of catastrophe is always possible. Yet thinking catastrophe, if catastrophe is upped - since the Middle East has experienced catastrophe for many years and is in the midst of a series of catastrophes as I speak - those who wish for catastrophe should be willing to pay the price with their own lives and treasure. Thus a warning for those who seek to push back Israel by way of catastrophe. In the Middle East and Israel-Palestine especially, the catastrophe could mean mutual destruction. If, afterward, there is a last man or woman standing it may not be worth his or her survival. So, for my exploration, by permanent I mean over the next years, certainly my lifetime and beyond, for the next fifty or one hundred years. As well, the scenarios for reversal of the permanent occupation I hear now, I heard thirty years ago: if only the world knew; if only Americans knew; the Arab world will rise up; Israel will collapse of its contradictions; demographics will win the day. Meanwhile, the occupation is consolidated.

Regardless of the length of time, whether it is twenty or fifty or hundred years or until the end of time, whatever the end of time can mean today, Jewish life has been and is now permanently scarred by the occupation of Palestine and Palestinians. To those who ask whether Jews, after the Holocaust, can participate in ethnic cleansing, our answer is hardly theoretical. Historically, factually, the answer is: "Like others before and after us, yes, after the Holocaust, in the creation and expansion of Israel, Jews are ethnic cleansers, too." To those who ask whether Jews, after the Holocaust, can participate in state sponsored and systematic, planned, terrorism, our answer is hardly theoretical. Historically, factually, the answer is: "Like others before and after us, yes, after the Holocaust, in the creation and expansion of Israel, Jews are participants in and enablers of state sponsored and systematic planned terrorism." These historical and factual statements amount to a confession that I made in Jerusalem thirty years ago and I make again this evening: "What we as Jews have done to you, the Palestinian people, is wrong. What we as Jews are doing to you, the Palestinian people, is wrong." Like the occupation of Palestine and Palestinians, this confession is obvious. It is also permanent. And how much more obvious and permanent it is today than it was decades ago.

However one parses our permanent occupation of Palestine and Palestinians, Jewish identity, whether religious, spiritual or secular, is now permanently infected with atrocity. I first wrote of this in 1997 in *Unholy Alliance: Religion and Atrocity in Our Time.* That was the title my publisher gave the book; marketing experts have their say. Yet when I think of *Unholy Alliance*, I first think of the title I gave the book and which is relevant to my lecture this evening: *Atrocity and the Language of God.* My book is less about how religion and power come together in atrocity, others have covered that territory and been heartily rewarded for it. Rather my book is about how atrocity, mass death but also genocide and ethnic cleansing, leads to and is in intrinsically bound up with distortions in language and religion. After mass death, genocide and ethnic cleansing, the language these horrors were carried out in carry the trauma it enabled. So, too, with religion that blesses atrocity.

In *Atrocity and the Language of God*, I began with the Holocaust and the scholarly work on the effects Nazism has had on the German language and religion. Then, I extended my analysis to Hebrew. After all, the ethnic cleansing of Palestinians in the formation and expansion of Israel was carried out in many languages, including Hebrew, and modern Hebrew was formed within the events that brought about and sustains the state of Israel. Since that time Israeli state policies, religious beliefs and political rhetoric that have brought ruin to Palestinians have been thought, spoken and executed in Hebrew. This once restricted and sacred language emerged into the history of the Jewish state with a violence that continues as I speak. Can such a language escape the distortions that atrocity mandates? In the formation, sustenance and expansion of Israel, Judaism and Jewish identity have likewise been actively employed, indeed have been militarized and, yes, infected with atrocity. Because once religion and identity become accomplices to atrocity they must disguise that atrocity and twist it to conform to an innocence and redemption that is now visited, as a form of oppression, on the Other, in this case the Palestinian people.[2]

True, no identity or religion is free of wrongheadedness, injustice and violence. Judaism, Jews and Jewish identity have existed in many and varied contexts over a long history. Yet the situation of modern Jewry is arguably distinct in Jewish history. Rarely, if ever before, has there been a collective Jewish empowerment to the extent we see it today. That empowerment is found in the status, freedom and access to venues of power that Jews have within at least two empire formations, the United States and Israel. And this within an almost global sense of Jewish entitlement and international indebtedness, for anti-Semitism, the Holocaust and thus the recognized need for Jewish empowerment in a state formation.

While arguments can be made for a lack of Jewish innocence before the emergence of the state of Israel, the situation of post-Holocaust Jewry and its now permanent entanglement with the empowered state of Israel, makes the situation unique. Too, Judaism and Hebrew, being upfront in empowered Jewish life and across the Jewish spectrum, has taken the loss of Jewish innocence to another level. The permanence of the situation places previous eras of Jewish empowerment on the back burner. Where else in

Jewish history, for example, do we find rabbinical students in a faraway land, America, required to spend a year or more in Israel imbibing its culture and learning the language of Hebrew as central to their Jewish identity? This in a Jewish state formed in the ethnic cleansing of an indigenous people with a powerful military armed with nuclear weapons.

The issue remains: What are Jews to do with the permanent occupation that leaves Jewish identity permanently infected with atrocity? Christians have dealt with this issue or should have. After all, in many ways the dominant form of Christianity most Christians inherit today thrived within atrocity. How else would Christianity have gone global? Unfortunately even those victims of an atrocity-filled Christianity now carry that very same Christianity deep within their interior life. Most of the world's Christians have been, as I wrote in *Atrocity and the Language of God*, "conquered by the Gospel." I also suggested there that these "historical Gospels" be read regularly in church - the Gospel of 1492, the Gospel of Colonialism, the Gospel of Auschwitz, all with their special "unholy" readings. On the Jewish side, I think of the Jewish cycle of Torah readings. The obvious congruent voice would be readings from the Book of Palestine.

Like other books of the Hebrew Bible, the Book of Palestine is fascinating. It is less a linear history as we might study in a primer on the history of Israel-Palestine. Rather, in the Book of Palestine, like other books in the Jewish canon, we find a creative narrative, full of the unexpected, with seemingly random appearances, disappearances and silences, then words spoken out of sequence and out of turn. God appears, mostly from the sideline, a God who was once in full flower, a diminished God known by name in the Book of Palestine as *I AM*, Who Was. Or sometimes, when God is named in a more positive vein, when God is present rather than AWOL, God's name resounds, *I AM*, Who Loves The Prophets. When parsing Israel's history we read of the ethnic cleansing of Palestine. There are words from Edward Said on exile and return, and from other Palestinians, like Naim Ateek, who narrates a section of his

Palestinian theology of liberation, his story of expulsion and how he found his voice. Palestinians report being tortured by Israelis speaking Hebrew. Jewish leaders in America describe these reports as forms of anti-Semitism. Other Jews ask: Could this be true? Descriptions of settlements abound, as do stories of Palestinian resistance. Jerusalem appears frequently in the Book of Palestine, as it is imagined, whole and just, and as it exists in real life, divided and unjust. A Jewish Theology of Liberation comes briefly on the scene. Some Jews jeer. Others embrace its arrival. A fascinating and disturbing image flashes before us: In the Ark of the Covenant the Torah scrolls are gone, replaced by Star of David Helicopter Gunships. There's no word if the Torah scrolls return. Early and later in the Book of Palestine we read of Palestinians martyred at the hands of Israeli soldiers. We hear Jews of Conscience cry out in the dead of night. They mourn the end of ethical Jewish history. Palestinian mothers grieve and fathers, too. Palestine is falling. Destruction is the order of the day. What is to be done?[3]

If my rendering of parts of the Book of Palestine seems far afield from the issue before us - if the occupation is permanent, is an ethical Jewish future possible - think again. For the prophetic, including its translation in the Rabbinic era, has set the ethical trajectory of Jewish life from its beginning. The issue has never been ethical perfection - is the Jewish community as a whole living an ethical life - but rather the possibility of a personal and communal ethical life has been the benchmark of Jewish destiny. For if not an ethical people, at least in aspiration, why be Jewish? And if not an ethical people, at least in aspiration, how to come close to a God who demands justice as the only way to belief?

Whether Jews are in fact an ethical people or, in a related way, chosen for a special destiny, is arguable. That the sacred scriptures Jews affirm and the formation of Jewish identity through time has revolved around ethics and chosenness is unarguable. There is no "Jewish" without these conceptual categories that demand implementation in real life. There is no time in Jewish history when Jews, in one way or another, have thought themselves like the Other Nations, except in a negative way. when the prophets accuse the people Israel of diverting from Jewish destiny. Jews have always felt themselves singled out among the nations for a special destiny and in a special relation with God, even and especially when God seems to be asleep at the wheel or AWOL. So, yes, against the grain of post-modern thought, Jewish exceptionalism is the bedrock of Jewish existence.

Problematic to some and for good reason, the ultimate question in Jewish life is in what direction this sense of exceptionalism leads us - to embrace a solidarity with the prophetic tradition for ourselves and in relation to others or to use that exceptionalism over against and as oppressive to our own ethical values and to others. In sum, an ethical Jewish future, at least as an aspiration, is a command. It is essential to the very future of the Jewish people. This is why the contradictions of contemporary Jewish life are extreme and why a Jewish civil war, down and dirty, is being fought today. If an ethical Jewish future was not at stake, as the proper and highest stake of what it means to be Jewish, why not simply accept our new found power as a good to be used however we want and need to? If an ethical Jewish future was not at stake, as the proper and highest stake of what it means to be Jewish, how does one explain, in the midst of Jewish flourishing and power, the emergence of Jews of Conscience, the identifiable heirs of the Jewish prophets?

Holocaust theology, the theology pioneered by my teacher, Richard Rubenstein, and others such as Elie Wiesel, Emil Fackenheim and Rabbi Irving Greenberg, was structured around remembrance of the Holocaust and support for Jewish empowerment, most especially in the state of Israel. These theologians saw support for Israel as a political and religious communal command after the Holocaust. Holocaust theology is complex, with a number of moving parts, but central to it is the warning against the application of the Jewish prophetic to post-Holocaust Jewry and the state of Israel. The fear of Holocaust theologians? That the Jewish prophetic, so central to Jewish life over the millennia, in fact the essence of

Jewish life from its origins, if applied to the state of Israel, would undermine Israel and eventually lead to its destruction. This is why Rabbi Irving Greenberg cautioned that a prophetic critique of Israel was the excommunicable sin of our era.[4]

Yet, just as Holocaust theologians warned against the return of the Jewish prophetic, it happened, is happening. In a time of unparalleled Jewish empowerment an ongoing explosion of the Jewish prophetic, focused directly and relentlessly on the unethical policies of the state of Israel in relation to the Palestine and Palestinians, is occurring. In light of Holocaust theology, prophetic Jews, Jews of Conscience, in Israel, America and beyond, risk excommunication and exile from the Jewish community. The penalties are extreme, from charges of self-hate and encouraging anti-Semitism and laying the groundwork for another Holocaust, to online stalking, disappearing job opportunities and more. The question before us, then, is why Jews speak out regardless of the penalties involved. On the one hand, it could be simply a matter of justice, righting the wrong Israel is committing against Palestine and Palestinians. It is that and something more. I believe what Jews of Conscience rail against and give their lives for is the loss of the possibility of a Jewish ethical future - without which there is no "Jewish." Jews of Conscience are fighting a high stakes battle against the final Jewish assimilation to unjust power which, in their view, articulated in overt Jewish language or not, signals the end of Jewish history.

Many years ago, a noted Jewish scholar, was asked about the issue of intermarriage in Jewish life. For many in the Jewish community the marriage of Jews with non-Jews foretells a dwindling of the Jewish population and Jewish commitment. The scholar's response was interesting and pertinent to my thoughts here. He said that though every Jew who marries a non-Jew has their own story, often that he or she simply fell in love with a non-Jew and that was that, the aggregate number of such cases represents an unconscious desire to be at home in the broader non-Jewish culture. Thus, intermarriage is less a personal choice than a Jewish desire for security and acceptance. Perhaps, too, this safety valve represents a desire to escape some of the external and internal pressures associated with being Jewish.

Whatever one makes of intermarriage, the issue of assimilation in Jewish history is longstanding and complex. So, too, is my argument that the explosion of the Jewish prophetic in our time, against all odds and every prohibition, is a refusal of a final assimilation, assimilation to injustice. For Jews of Conscience to come into solidarity with Palestinians is to cross every redline in normative Jewish life. Jews of Conscience who did so decades ago fled the Jewish community, have no association with it and, if asked, have primarily negative opinions about Jewish life in general. What in God's name has brought so many of these Jews back into the Jewish arena if not as a heart and soul protest against the crossing of this ultimate redline of injustice? Still, it is doubtful that the protest against assimilation to injustice will succeed. The injustice of Israel toward Palestinians is permanent. Can we say the same for prophetic protest?

Theologically speaking, the prophetic has its own existence. Once having arrived in history during Biblical times, the prophetic periodically makes its presence felt. In earlier times, God was at the command but more recently God is questioned and often dismissed. The prophetic remains, perhaps as a witness to the *I AM*, Who Was. Regardless of how we explain the perseverance of the prophetic, we know the prophetic when we see it. We see it now. Yet the prophetic fails; history rarely changes course. Rather history evolves in various directions. The straight lines of the prophetic can be drawn historically, yet they remain on the margins of history's canvas. Jews, like humankind in general, can endure only so much of the prophetic. In the case of Israel-Palestine, the permanent occupation and permanent infection of Jewish life with atrocity, will continue.

The exploding prophetic of our time will fail. It already has. This means that the great Jewish witnesses found in the Book of Palestine, those already mentioned, and others like Martin Buber,

Hannah Arendt, B'Tselem, Jewish Voice for Peace, as well the new non-Zionist congregation, Tzedek Chicago, will likewise fail. They already have. Whatever happens in the future, whether their witness is listened to often or at all, what they want and believe will only, and this if they are lucky, factor into something they cannot accept or has not been expected. For the Book of Palestine is a witness document not a political roadmap. It is read as a lament and a hope. As a testimony, too, a documentation as it were, of the end of ethical Jewish history, at least as we have known and inherited it. Alas, the Jewish prophetic has consistently documented our end. It is doing so as I speak.

The Jewish prophetic will survive; it will continue to accompany and haunt those Jews who enable and perpetuate injustice against Palestinians. These Jewish enablers of injustice - I call them Constantinian Jews - will triumph. But the Jewish narrative of innocence and redemption so important to post-Holocaust Jewish identity will not survive the prophetic insurgency. In fact, on this, rather than the political front, the Jewish narrative for the future has already been decided. Without the claim of ethics and justice, the memory of the Holocaust recedes and instead becomes an accusatory image used against Jewish claims on the world. Israel, once a point of pride, influence and status increasingly becomes a liability in the Jewish and broader public discourse. Having ceded the ethical high ground, Constantinian Jewry in Israel, America and beyond will negotiate the Jewish future by extending their power over against Palestinians, Jews of Conscience and others who challenge Israeli policies. Jews of Conscience will continue to agitate, witness and lose, though not completely and not forever.

There will come a time when Jews of Conscience negotiate the prophetic. The Jewish civil war is the first step of the negotiation between prophetic and Constantinian Jews over the Jewish future. Whether the children and grandchildren of Jews of Conscience will continue the struggle is unknown. Constantinian Jews have political and financial reasons to hone their message. For the most part, Jews of Conscience have only exile to call their home. Duration is a factor here as Constantinian Jews have more strategic depth than Jews of Conscience. The difficulties of exile wear on the exiled and their children. The prophetic is the deepest embrace of Jewish life; it is the only reason to be Jewish. Still, hardship and the permanence of defeat may make the prophetic less and less viable as a way of life. The only way for Jews of Conscience to survive the Jewish civil war and carry on their witness is in exile, an exile that deepens by the day in Israel, America and beyond. Like the occupation and Jewish history infected by atrocity, this exile is permanent. The trauma of injustice and assault that Jews of Conscience experience by the Constantinian Jewish establishments in Israel and America are longstanding and deep. They increase by the day as well.[5]

Exiles always think they are returning home. Mostly they don't and if they do the landscape is so changed they return to a foreign country. Jewish Israelis who leave the physical space of Israel or the cultural space while remaining in Israel are gone for good. Jews in America who leave the Jewish community are gone for good. Already, the primary community for Jewish exiles are with other exiles from other religions, cultures and nationalities. I call this community the New Diaspora. In the New Diaspora, Jews mingle with other displaced people, lick their wounds, protest injustice and try to salvage the shattered remains of the tradition they grew up within. In the New Diaspora, no overarching symbolic, cultural or religious structure is desired. Rather, the community comes together in an openness to the spirit and the struggle for justice.

Many Jews are already in the New Diaspora, finding life among the ruins, but naming the final exile in the New Diaspora is still in process. Naming the New Diaspora reality is as difficult as the exile itself; it is like anticipating, then hearing, the final bell tolling. Exiles tend to delay what will come soon enough. Many Palestinians reside in the New Diaspora as well. Here Jews and Palestinians forge important bonds of justice seeking and mutual support. Sometimes in exile within Israel-Palestine and often outside it, the lessons of the harsh history between Jews and Palestinians are hashed out, aspects of a divisive history are acknowledged and overcome. A revolutionary forgiveness is approached. Mutual solidarity becomes the watchword; an injury to one becomes an injury to the Other—who is no longer Other. The hope of many was that revolutionary forgiveness could begin in Jerusalem, with a confession from Israel and move to a program of sharing Jerusalem - joint governance, shared education, integrated policing and grocery shopping, in theory and practice a shared life of Jews and Palestinians. For our permanent moment, at least, that shared life has begun in the New Diaspora. Will that witness one day become a homecoming?

I end with a contradiction or perhaps a fulfillment. I ask you to be the judge. Perhaps it was a coincidence that when I wrote my Jewish theology of liberation, my oldest son, Aaron, was coming to life. Or it may have been a subconscious sense that I was preparing to hand down what it means to be Jewish to my children. Since that that time, Aaron, and his brother, Isaiah, have become my life companions. So in closing, I share with you the fragments of Jewishness that Aaron has inherited and articulated in response to my life's journey.

The first is a definition of the prophetic Aaron wrote as a commentary of the occasion of the 25th anniversary of the Spanish edition of my Jewish theology of liberation: "Indeed, I have inherited an interpretive framework and existential directedness, a way of life toward which to strive. I have been given the tools with which I may now seek an intentional orientation toward myself; toward various communities, my own included; toward others; toward the Other; toward the divine; toward the world." The second, and here I close, is Aaron's response to elements of my lecture via social media. Note that Aaron and other young Jews of Conscience are up for the challenge I present in this lecture. Aaron writes: "Despite all the plans cementing the occupation, millions of Palestinians' steadfastness and increased international awareness and activism and divestment and more, all point to a possible future. History has a way of moving and shaking the foundations of expectations.

41

Doomed to destruction? I don't think so. One democratic state. Equal rights for all. Is on its way. Which doesn't mean by the way, that Judaism is any more redeemable than Christianity after the Holocaust. All I am saying is that it will happen in my lifetime."[6]

Notes

1. *Toward a Jewish Theology of Liberation* was first published by Orbis Books in 1987. The second edition, also by Orbis, was published in 1989. See the third and expanded edition, *Toward a Jewish Theology of Liberation: The Challenge of the 21st Century* (Waco: Baylor University Press, 2004).

2. *Unholy Alliance: Religion and Atrocity in Our Time* (Minneapolis: Fortress, 1997).

3. For my first take on the naming of God, see my "I AM, Who Loves the Prophets, Loves You: A Meditations on the Progressive/Prophetic at the End of Jewish History," in Susanne Scholz, ed., *God Loves Diversity and Justice: Progressive Scholars Speak About Faith Politics and the World* (Lanham, Maryland: Lexington Books, 2013), 57-70.

4. Rabbi Irving Greenberg sets forth the parameters of prophetic thought and the penalties to be applied in our age of Jewish empowerment in his essay, "The Ethics of Jewish Power," in *Beyond Occupation: American Jewish, Christian and Palestinian Voices for Peace*, ed. Rosemary Radford Ruether and Marc H. Ellis (Boston: Beacon Press, 1990), 22-74.

5. For an extended discussion of these issues see my *Finding Our Voice: On the Prophetic and Other Misadventures*, forthcoming.

6. For Aaron's commentary see my "La Herencia de Hacer Que Dios Exista; Respuesta de un Hijo" in Marc H. Ellis, *Hacia Una Teologia Judia De La Liberacion* (Edicion Especial, 25 Aniversario 1988-2014), ed. and trans. Maria Del Mar Rosa-Rodriguez (San Juan, Puerto Rico: Editorial Isla Negra, 263-270.